"With all my love to
"The Pigges"
Fern S.

A Grandma's Letters to God

Ruth Youngdahl Nelson

A Grandma's Letters to God

AUGSBURG Publishing House • Minneapolis

A GRANDMA'S LETTERS TO GOD

Copyright © 1983 Augsburg Publishing House.

Scripture quotations unless otherwise noted are from the Revised Standard Version of the Bible, copyright 1946, 1952, and 1971 by the Division of Christian Education of the National Council of Churches.

Scripture quotations marked TEV in this publication are from the Good News Bible, Today's English Version, copyright 1966, 1971, 1976 by American Bible Society. Used by permission.

Scripture quotations marked Phillips are from The New Testament in Modern English, copyright 1958 by J. B. Phillips.

Library of Congress Cataloging in Publication Data

Nelson, Ruth Youngdahl.
   A GRANDMA'S LETTERS TO GOD.

   1. Prayers. 2. Nelson, Ruth Youngdahl. I. Title.
BV245.N46 1984   242   83-72109
ISBN 0-8066-2053-6

Manufactured in the U.S.A.   APH 10-2886

    3   4   5   6   7   8   9   0   1   2   3   4   5   6   7   8   9

To all children everywhere,
this grandma dedicates these letters.
It is her prayer that the beautiful
world God has created may be preserved,
that all people may learn to live
in peace and reconciliation,
with justice and food for everyone!

Acknowledgments

I want to thank Karl Lempp, my grandson, who meticulously read my careless handwriting and typed these pages for me. It was a real labor of love!

And thank you to Inge, Karl, and Biz for their illustrations. It was the cooperation of the whole family that made possible this writing during my stay in their home in Bernhausen, West Germany.

Preface

For years the little volumes entitled *Children's Letters to God* have been an inspiration to me. The opening prayer in one of them is as succinct as the most theological observation. A young boy writes, "Dear God, count me in!"

As the years have lengthened and "the keepers of the house tremble . . . and the grinders cease because they are few, and those that look through the windows are dimmed . . . and one rises up at the voice of a bird . . ." (Eccles. 12:3-4), so has my soul come full circle—to the simple trust of a little child, to a warm, direct, loving relationship with an ever-present God. This is what I'd like to share in these letters, for as I write I shall be praying them.

A world without God—I shudder at the thought. And yet it seems to me our values are eliminating God, collectively and individually, except to give God a passing nod in public places.

Please God, use the words that follow!

10

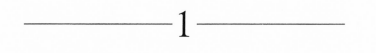

1

Dear God,

How glad I am that to you I do not have to give any credentials or biographical information. You know everything there is to know about me, inside and out. And I don't have to introduce myself because we've been in communication for a long time, especially in the nocturnal hours when sleep has passed over my bedroom, and I've been left wide-eyed in the darkness of the night.

And just yesterday as I watched wave after wave of little birds like an unfurling ribbon against the blue of the sky, little birds flying south to be protected from the harsh wintry winds, I commented to my daughter Biz, "Just think! God knows every sparrow that falls!" This knowledge is too great for my understanding, but that's the wonder of who you are and the magnitude of your love.

Sometimes I lose sight of this and grovel with ulcer-producing anxiety. What I want in these letters, Lord, is to unburden again, to ask for wisdom and guidance, to talk about the problems in today's tumultuous world—and to receive the solutions you would give us.

This tumultuous world! What amazing changes

have happened over the span of my years! Radio, television, air travel, and now space exploration. Should I be hopeless or hopeful? What does it look like to you?

I remember when, as a young girl, I put the first set of radio earphones to my ears. I thought that was a miracle — to hear music from miles away without any obvious mechanical connection. And now, how much has followed! How little we know of the wonders of your creation! Yet how proud we are of "our" achievements!

A cartoon I saw just today illustrates how confused we are. The picture showed a man in a computer center asking the salesman, "Do you have one that can help me decide which is the one for me?" I'm frightened, Lord, when I think of man-made mechanisms taking over.

But I take comfort in the thought that the basics of life don't change! Your love is forever and ever! What that meant to my father and mother, my grandparents, and previous generations is the same as what it means to my family and to me. I'm grateful that as the years have unfolded in my life, so has my knowledge of you and my understanding of the magnitude of your love and mercy. There have been times when I've tried to box you in and fashion you according to my narrow, selfish concept! And, O Lord, how I thank you for revealing yourself in a way that I can better understand, in your coming to earth in the person of your Son, Jesus Christ. He said, "Anyone who has seen me,

has seen the Father," that you and he are one. And I thank you for your promised Spirit who is ever-present to guide and teach and comfort and challenge. The mystery of it, Lord, is beyond my understanding, but the reality of it is my faith.

Thank you for your patient listening. Thank you for being love! I love you!

Ruth

2

Dear God,

What a wonderful thing is the body you've created for me! And you have told us that it is the temple of your Spirit! That makes it holy! Yet sometimes I treat it so shabbily! I eat things that aren't good for my body, and often I eat too much. When Biz pulls out of the oven a pan of her delectable Danish puff, I'm sunk! I not only taste it; I devour much more than I should, and then I live with a heavy stomach!

I don't give my body a chance to rest as much as it needs. Now I awaken early in the morning, so I should go to bed earlier, but I'm afraid I'll miss out on something. And I don't exercise as I ought to. In the very fabric of your creation there are rules to follow for healthy, alive bodies. Help me, Lord, to be better disciplined, more ready to follow your directions.

Thank you for helping me through this last heart attack. Thank you for my loving family who were so helpful. It isn't that I'm afraid to die! Often I think how wonderful it will be when you tap me on the shoulder. It's the pain of the process of dying that is tough. And I've discovered how easy it is to tell others you'll give grace to bear what comes but how hard, when the pain hits me, to remember that.

Sometimes when I come from visiting elderly folks in the seriously ill ward, I am very puzzled. You know how many times I've asked you "Why don't you take them home, Lord?" I guess I want to play God.

But that old man's prayer in Psalm 71 finds its echo in many hearts, including my own. I cry out: "Lord, I put my hope in you; I have trusted in you since I was young. I have relied on you all my life. . . . Now that I am old and my hair is gray, do not abandon me, O God! Be with me while I proclaim your power and might to all generations to come" (Ps. 71:5-6, 18 TEV). Lord, let my witness in these closing years of my life be one of faith that produces hope and hope that generates love! Help me not to forever be talking about my aches and pains nor thinking about myself! Let my grandchildren see your love not only sustaining me but also sending me on my way rejoicing!

They saw it in their grandfather when his days were drawing to an end. To the very last, he was fun to be with despite the cancer through his whole body and his badly damaged heart. I remember in the hospital how he kidded about taking the female hormone estrogen. He teasingly said: "Is my voice changing? Are my breasts developing?" It must have been your presence that gave him such twinkling courage!

Growing old isn't easy, Lord! It's hard to acknowledge that there are things you can't do now that you always took for granted. But help me to flavor with grace the things I can do and to know the words you said to Joshua are for me, too! "Do not be afraid or discouraged, for I, the Lord your God, am with you wherever you go" (Josh. 1:9 TEV). "I will always be with you; I will never abandon you" (Josh. 1:5 TEV).

So who's afraid of the lengthening years? Thank you for these promises!

> Your aging daughter,
> *Ruth*

3

Dear God,

Early this morning, as I lay in bed, I thought again about the passing of time. I recalled some of the things your Word says about it—how "a thousand years to you are like one day; they are like yesterday, already gone, like a short hour in the night" (Ps. 90:4 TEV).

You have told us there is a time for everything (Eccles. 3:1), and you have exhorted us to make "the most of the time, because the days are evil" (Eph. 5:16). Yes, our days pass "swifter than a weaver's shuttle" (Job 7:6). Help me not to waste time, Lord, but also give me the grace to know I'm not wasting it when I'm listening to you and searching your Word, that I don't always have to be *doing*. Give me the perspective of the poet who said, "Each day is a little life!"

How I need discernment, Lord. Please guide me in the use of my time. Often the choice is not between something good or bad, but between two things that seem equally good. One of your children said that when she was faced with such a choice she would ask herself, "Is it for God, or is it for me?" Sometimes that's a hard choice.

Thank you for my mother's teaching: "As your day, so shall your strength be." We really need to remember that as we grow old and not fret about what the future might hold. That's what made the songwriter say:

> Our times are in Your hand;
> O God we wish them there.
> Our lives, our souls, our friends
> We leave entirely to Your care.

I remember reading about a farmer who said, "I live as if I were going to die tonight, and farm as if I would live forever." I guess that's what you mean when you tell us to make the most of the time for the days are evil.

Some of your children, West Indies refugees in London, taught us simple, happy songs that have been so helpful. We asked them how they could be so joyful when things looked so bleak — they were in a strange country far from home, without jobs, not knowing what the future might hold. Their response was, "We have some songs that will tell you!" Your presence in them, Lord, was so obvious when they sang:

> The time to be happy is now;
> The place to be happy is here;
> The way to be happy is to make someone
>   happy
> and you'll have a bit of heaven down here!

They had another song that went this way:

> If you know the Lord is leading you,
> What are you going to worry about?
> If you know the Lord is leading you,
> Why don't you sing and shout?
> Sing, "Glory hallelujah," praise his name;
> Every day is just the same.
> If you know the Lord is leading you,
> What are you going to worry about?

That's what you've told us. "Have no anxiety about tomorrow."

Help me, Lord, to hear you and to trust!

Ruth

4

Dear God,

Thanks! Thanks from an overflowing heart! I saw one of your terrific answers to prayer yesterday. You always answer; I just don't always recognize the answer. But yesterday I couldn't miss it!

I told you about Willy a year ago—the young student at the *Sprachenkolleg* (a language college) in Stuttgart. He was learning Latin, Hebrew, and Greek before entering the theological school in Tübingen. Willy had grown up in an orphanage; both his parents had died when he was a child. Some way or another this bright boy had suffered the trauma of the uncertainties of life and had developed a stuttering handicap. But here he was preparing to go into the ministry! Biz and I pledged to each other to make Willy our prayer concern.

Since our first meeting, Willy has been pursuing his studies at Tübingen University. Last night he dropped by with his girl friend—and you know what? There's hardly a trace of stuttering—even when he speaks English (and to him that's a foreign language)! His face was radiant, reflecting the freedom he feels. Thanks, Lord! Thanks for what you are doing for Willy!

Forgive me because I so often come supplicating

and so little of the time return to give thanks! I remember the story of the lepers whom you healed (Luke 17:12-19). There were 10 and only one returned to express his gratitude. That's a really low average, one out of 10. But I'm afraid that's fairly common.

The book of Psalms is full of thanksgiving for your loving mercy. We are enjoined to "give thanks to the Lord, because he is good; his love is eternal" (Ps. 106:1 TEV). And another psalmist talks about how all your works shall give thanks to you (Ps. 145:10)!

And when Jesus was bodily on this earth, he gave thanks before everything he did. Yes, in the breaking of the bread, he gave thanks.

How careless we who call ourselves by your name have become! How slow we are to acknowledge that all good things come from you.

We should ask ourselves how often we thank the folks who have prepared our food. I wonder how many people sit down to a meal in a restaurant and unashamedly bow their heads in gratitude for your provision. What a time to remember those who are serving and the cooks in the kitchen! It is your gracious provision that makes it all possible. You know, Lord, something special happens when I do this. Barriers are broken down, and the rapport between the one who waits on me and myself becomes a happy exchange of friendliness. And what a help to the digestion! When I eat with joy and gratitude there is a wholeness of the body that assimilates and uses to the full the nourishment it receives. You have wonderfully created us!

Today, now, Lord, give me grace to be thankful for everything!

Ruth

5

Dear God,

This is a call for help! Massive, worldwide, cataclysmic help! Nothing but the victorious power of your presence can save us. I'm writing about us as individuals, as a church, as a nation, and as the world. You'll have to bear with several letters! I can't get enough in one, and it's really a matter of life and death! You know all about it, but I must pour out my heart to you anyway. That's what you have told us to do!

It's this, Lord: Our values are all topsy-turvy. We're striving for the things that perish. Each person needs to ask in his or her own heart, "What's my priority? Who is first in my life?" The subtle craft of the evil one is so wily that he can blind our judgment to the point that we make even something that is good become an idol. We do this when it becomes the most important thing.

I struggle not to love my children more than I love you. I have a rough time bringing my concerns for them to you in prayer, trusting you to do what's best for them. I want you to do what I think. I want life to be easy for them; I want them to have a comfortable living and good homes and the right education and promising jobs. I want people to like them, especially those who can promote them. The mother of two of Christ's disciples had ambitions, too! She aimed for them to be closest to you. Is it wrong to want good for my children; for my husband? Maybe we'd better consider what "good" is. Maybe we'd better think about trusting you for that, you who see the end from the beginning!

Lord, we need a new direction in our lives. We've been worshiping affluence and success and comfort

and status and possessions! The attaining of these so often motivates us. Where does such a course end?

I am haunted by the remembrance of two ignominious deaths in recent years. There are countless others, but these particularly come to mind: Howard Hughes and Elvis Presley. The former accumulated enough money to eat him up and in the end destroy him. What a pitiable, lonely, desperate effort he made with his billions to evade death! What a contrast his life was to that of your child, St. Francis of Assisi, who sold all his wealth and went about in the beauty of your creation, serving the poor. How he has enriched all of us with his life and prayers!

Elvis Presley used your gift of voice to amass millions, to feed on adulation, and in the end, really, to destroy his own life! What a travesty that so many people have worshiped him!

Call us to our senses, Lord, in our mad pursuits. Help us to hear you when you ask: "Will a person gain anything if he wins the whole world but loses his life?" (Matt. 16:26 TEV). And again: "Be concerned above everything else with the Kingdom of God and with what he requires of you, and he will provide you with all these other things" (Matt. 6:33 TEV).

Please help me, God, to get my values straight!

Ruth

6

Dear God,

Yesterday as I was worshiping in the little chapel here in Germany, I thought about all the places around the world where, in huge cathedrals and little chapels and homes, people were gathered to praise you and seek your guidance. I wonder what we look like to you. Are we what you want us to be? Are we the yeast of love you mean us to be? Do our programs indicate that our basic concerns are not what you will do for us, but rather what we can be and do for others?

It's so easy and tempting, Lord, to fall into the world's pattern of socializing and entertaining. There's nothing wrong with having fun, but should that be the main purpose of your people? Are we more interested in what will attract many people than in whether or not you are at the center of all we do, of finding how to live out your love in the community and to the ends of the earth? Is the community different because we are there?

I've been thinking, too, about our budget. How much do we gather to spend on ourselves? Surely you don't want your house of prayer to be ugly or uncared for. But should we make that our main objective? Should the largest part of our ingatherings go to maintaining the home base? What is the mission of your church, this body of believers?

I've been reading about the early church, and, as one writer said, "They undoubtedly had something today's church has lost." What a story it is, Lord! A little band of ordinary people impregnated and infused a pagan worldly society with a new transforming power — your spirit and love. It wasn't easy; it meant putting their lives on the line. And many were martyred. How sleazy many of our activities today must look to you! How afraid we are of taking any stand that might cause controversy!

There's this situation in South Africa and Namibia, where black people and Indian people are considered to be less than those born of the so-called white race. Namibia, that gallant little country in South West Africa, has literally become a slave state. The church has suffered terrible persecution. Just recently its printing press was destroyed and burned. We're tempted to ask, "Where are you, Lord, to let these things happen?" Then we remember — we are your agents! We could put human rights before the "almighty" dollar and remove any investments we have. Our pension board, our seminary funds, our churches' investments should never have the taint of putting the profit before the cause. Raise up in our midst prophets who will dare to speak out for the causes of righteousness!

Sometimes the secular world leads the way and sets the example. Hurray for the state of Massachusetts for passing a law that withdrew all state funds from South Africa because of its unjust human rights practices! We need to listen to you when you say, "If my people who are called by my name humble themselves, and pray and seek my face, and turn from their wicked ways, then I will hear from heaven, and will forgive their sin . . ." (2 Chron. 7:14).

Help us, God!

Ruth

<hr>

7

Dear God,

Yesterday I wrote to you about the church, but when I finished that letter, there were many things I still wanted to say. I want to talk about some of the places I know where your Spirit has broken through. Even as I write this, I'm aware that in every church you have your "little flock"—those who are the "yeast," who are not satisfied to use as their measuring stick: "What did we do last year?" And come to think of it, in every soul, somewhere deep down, there is your spark! Help me not to be judgmental, and erase any vestige of spiritual pride. Where would I be, Lord, if it hadn't been for all those who have blessed my life and for your ever-lasting mercy?

But in different places there are those who gather for strength to launch out into service. My Augustana church is one like that! Lots of folks thought the old mother church should have moved out of the downtown area. A large part of the membership is over 60 years, with 170 people 80 years of age or older. Yet here they are, running an active, spirit-filled program for children gathered by buses, for Native Americans, for the elderly, as well as an Emergency Relief Center. Your love sprouts all over the place! And an especially nice part of it all is the cooperation and support that comes from suburban churches. Yes, there are witnesses to the Spirit's presence.

And I think of Bethel Church in Garfield Park, Chicago. That's a low-income area, but you are right there in their concern for others. How quick they were to help the Haitian refugees when they arrived. How generously they share the burdens and the challenge of their neighborhood! Their work with the elderly and their cooperative efforts are all an outflowing of your Holy Spirit. And the propelling power is prayer! What fun it is to sit in on a Bible study and witness how they listen to you and want to obey you.

I don't have much patience, Lord, with folks who run around to find a church that makes them the most comfortable! What you say to me is, "Where are you most needed?" What power there would be if each of us would try, by your grace, to make our church what you want it to be: your living, breathing presence of love in the community and to the ends of the earth; a prophetic voice that dares to speak against the evils of injustice, hunger, warmongering, and similar sins that are destroying the world. If, instead of quarreling with each other, we would unite as Christians, the world's climate would be changed! Begin with me!

You have said to us: "Why do you call me 'Lord, Lord,' and not do what I tell you?" (Luke 6:46). And before you ask that question, you ask some very strong things: "If you love only the people who love you, why should you receive a blessing?" (Luke 6:32 TEV). And again: "Love your enemies, do good to those who hate you" (Luke 6:27). You tell us to go the second mile; to turn the other cheek, yes, and to visit those in prison; to feed those who are hungry; to welcome those who are strangers (Matt. 25:31 ff.).

Your church, Lord, this body of believers should be your caring, throbbing, healing heart! Use me in that process! I want your love to shine through me!

Ruth

8

Dear God,

What infinite patience you need with me! I should think you'd give up! I did it again last night! I spent a couple of hours tossing and turning and taking aspirin, my mind in a dither and my body reflecting the tumult and the concern. Why does it take me so long to accept the solution you offer?

I think it was that book I read until the wee, small hours. Or was it those nuts I nervously gobbled? Both were foolishness! And all my own. About the book, it left me so distraught about the world and so churned up about our selfish pursuits and the insidious immorality of our not caring about other people's needs that I couldn't sleep. How easy it is for us who call ourselves Christians to harangue away at the obvious sins of others: adultery, drunkenness, drug addiction. How hard it is for us to see that our sins of complacency and lovelessness are just as great, if not greater, because we ought to know better!

The corruption, dishonesty, and "finagling" that goes on in government and public life, Lord, is very discouraging! All this was the inner turmoil that completely disintegrated my sleep. I was really desperate when I turned to you in prayer.

Then it happened—oh, but not all at once! I sat up in bed, resting my back on the big pillows. I had taken all the nitroglycerin I dared. But as I closed my eyes, I began thinking of all the people I wanted to bring to you. I remembered when Clarence and I visited Hulda, a 94-year-old friend in the "Home for the Incurables" (what a hideous name!), in Washington, D.C. Hulda's whole left side had been paralyzed by a stroke. After she had the stroke she told the visiting pastor, "Isn't it good, pastor, it didn't happen to the other side?"

Well, during our visit this time she told us how she had a hard time sleeping in the early morning hours. But then she remembered that Jesus had said, "O Jerusalem, Jerusalem, I would gather you in my arms as a mother gathers her chicks under her wings." "That's what I did, pastor," she said. "I thought of all the people in our church I could remember, and tucked each one under the wing of the Lord!"

Well, that's what happened to me last night. I began with my family, remembering each of them as I visualized them and thought of their needs. Then I thought of the circle of people around my family. I did this with Clarence's family and then with our church family and then in quietness waited for the Spirit to call to mind others. Without my realizing it, two hours went by, and as I glanced at the clock, I became conscious that my body was at rest; that the twitching and shifting had stopped; that my mind knew a beautiful peace—the peace that comes from resting in you. There came to mind the Bible verse I had learned in church school and

had always loved: "Call upon me in the day of trouble; I will deliver you, and you shall glorify me" (Ps. 50:15). And in later years: "Come to me, all who labor and are heavy laden, and I will give you rest" (Matt. 11:28).

Those are beautiful promises from you, God, and I thank you for them. They really work! Thanks!

Ruth

9

Dear God,

How shall I begin? I am so overloaded with concern about my beloved country! You are giving it such a tremendous opportunity to help make a new world—a world where there will be nobody needing to die of starvation, where every child born will have a decent chance to survive, where everybody will be treated like a first class citizen! My beloved country can take the leadership for such a goal.

And what are we doing, Lord, but putting our trust in the false god of power—physical, destructive power as is horribly represented in the nuclear proliferation; Trident submarines, MX missiles, and a whole barrage of monsters of destruction. Lord, how can I get people to understand that one Trident submarine has the power of 2040 Hiroshimas, that when Nobel invented dynamite he thought its destructive power was so terrible it would frighten people into never having another war? How little he calculated the evil nature in us all, our wanting to be God and trusting our judgment.

Trusting—there's the rub. Your Commandment says: "You shall have no other Gods before me" and constantly in your Word you tell us to *trust* you, no matter what. My beloved country is putting its trust in superior powers of destruction, in competing with the enemy, in the country with the greater arsenal. And we glibly use your name as if we were the chosen people! Lord, I wanted to vomit when I read that one prominent woman called the nuclear bomb your gift to America! What conception does she have of you? Does she think you are a God of death and destruction? Doesn't she see you on the cross, praying for your enemies? Doesn't she remember how you told Peter in the garden when he was wanting to defend you, that he should put away his sword, that your kingdom would never come by the sword?

What do we mean by the inscription on our coins: "In God we trust"? Help me to get the word out that those who put their trust in you will never be put to shame, that there is still time to halt this crazy course of destruction, that everybody counts! Keep me writing to my representatives in Congress and to my senators and to the president. Help me to do everything possible, nonviolently, to keep this horror from escalating!

I take comfort in the story of Jonah. Nineveh was a very wicked city, but you cared enough to want to redeem it. Jonah felt it should be destroyed and fled as far away as he could in the opposite direction. But you never give us up—nor did you him. In his place of desperation you caused him to turn to you in prayer—and you gave him another chance. Then the miracle happened! The people, including the king, repented and asked for mercy. And, loving God that you are, you changed your mind and gave them another chance! Why do folks fuss about the form of the story and forget what you are teaching in it: your love and concern for everybody, your everlasting mercy, the miracle of repentance? Guide us, Spirit of God, to your truth when we read. And in the midst of the horror and despair all around us, keep alive hope and love and trust in your wonder-working ways! You can even use me, Lord! Thanks!

Ruth

—————— 10 ——————

Dear God,

First of all, I want to say thank you, again, for listening! It's such a joy to be able to pour out to you the struggles and concerns that burden my heart. I'm afraid that too seldom do I share the joys and gratitude. And I know I don't have to tell you a thing. You know everything, even what I think. But I remember, Jesus, when you were on earth, you took time for everybody who came to you with their needs. So thank you again for listening.

I'm puzzled, Lord, about the paradox of the times in which we live. The world has become smaller and bigger. How can that be? Well, when I was a little girl, my world wasn't much bigger than Minnesota, and the people I knew were pretty much like my family and me. Oh, there were occasional glimpses into faraway places, like when the archbishop of Sweden visited Minneapolis and we got to meet him personally. But he was much like us, too. I can't remember as a child getting to know anybody from other races. Visiting missionaries told about them, but there were no personal contacts.

And economically, too, my world was pretty small. We had no "rich" friends (in terms of possessions), nor did we have any very poor ones. Oh, I remember peg-leg John thumping down 11th Avenue every spring and knocking at our door, and how my mother spread a white cloth on the table and treated him like a king. There was no back door handout! And I remember vaguely how when my father sold his grocery store, there were thousands of dollars owed by people who said they couldn't pay their bills, and he didn't have the heart to press them! But all of that was pretty remote from my homogenous, protected life. My world was very small.

And now, *wham!* The land, the seas, the skies have blown wide open our great big world—yes, and outer space too! It's overwhelming—and I'm having growing pains! Now the starving people around the world are my neighbors. Millions of starving people, including children who haven't enough nourishing food to keep them alive—and

our garbage cans are filled to overflowing and our standard of living keeps rising as we want more and more of the things that perish! Why, one man who was trying to help people farm in Central America told of how when babies were stillborn, the parents would rejoice because then the little ones become "angelettes" without having to suffer the pangs of starvation. And my country is spending billions for bombs to destroy and asking the farmers not to plant grain because we have such stockpiles of it. What does that look like to you? The earth is yours, and all that is in it, and there should be enough for everybody! What judgment will need to fall to awaken us? My world can be so selfishly small, but you've given me glimpses of some of the amazing people in what used to be faraway lands, and now I feel that not just my city, my state, my country, is my home, but the great, wide, world is my home, and all creatures are yours, and nobody is more important than anybody else.

I need to ask myself, God, "How big is my world?"

Ruth

Dear God,

What I talked to you about yesterday, Lord, is haunting me—the amazing world in which I live! And I've been thinking about some of the places I've been privileged to visit, and some of the fantastic scenes that glow in my mind, and some of the beautiful people who have enriched my life. I remember hearing the late Dr. E. Stanley Jones speak in St. Paul back in the 30s. What he said now finds its echo in my heart. "If I had a thousand lives to live," he said, "they wouldn't be enough to live in all the places I'd like to." Then he went on to say when he was in China, he thought of how he'd like to share you there; and when he was in Africa, he loved those people and wished he could serve there; and India was the place to which he had given most of his life, and where he felt he belonged; but when he came to America, this was the place of his birth, and he belonged here, too. That's the way I feel, Lord.

When people ask me, "Of all the places you've been, which do you like best?" I say, "The place where I am at this time." And that's the truth! I could live in any one of the places and feel at home and love the people. And love the people—I guess that's the key!—and then you're there! You're everywhere!

The Lempp family, who spent some 20 years in Indonesia, still longs to go back to that land of eternal summer. And not for the weather, but for the beautiful friends that became their family of God out there.

There was Mrs. Mazrie. She was a friend in Jakarta, married to a soldier. They had five children. You know how she devoted herself to your work and helped to teach children about you and your love. She hadn't been feeling well, so she went to the doctor. He examined her for some time and then sent her home. But when she got there, the door was locked. That surprised her, because she could hear members of the family inside. Finally they called out to her: "You can't come in because you have leprosy!" I wonder, Lord, what her thoughts were then!

She did the only thing she knew to do: she walked out to the government leprosarium some kilometers away and asked to enter. Alone, deserted by her family, a pariah on society—what next? Surely there must have been a deep lonely valley with the resounding echo of "Why?" But she didn't stay in that frame of mind long! Looking around her, she began asking herself what she could do for the Lord there. So she gathered the children for Sunday school and, with the aid of friends on the outside, helped with a Christian fellowship in that Muslim institution. Many years have passed and she is still there.

A postscript—a further indication of your presence in this amazing woman—is a story all its own. Her husband had taken another woman into his house to care for the children. When the children were grown, they made contact with their blood mother. Their father had died, and there was a pension from the army for his widow. Legally it was for our leper friend. But when the children urged her to take it, she said no. She felt the other woman should have it, because she had brought up the children. This is even more amazing when you know that the government's provision for these institutions is very limited, and often the woman doesn't have the wherewithal she needs to buy the medicine for her failing eyes.

She's become a part of my world and my prayers, Lord, and my life has been greatly enriched by knowing about her. Indonesia is a beautiful land of gorgeous flowers, exotic fruits, and flora and fauna, and I could live there with joy! But I love it most because there are people like Mrs. Mazrie there! Thank you for your great, wide, wonderful world!

Ruth

12

Dear God,

Last night I was reminded again of your great, wide world when we visited in the home of a German family who had lived in Hong Kong. In that missionary's eye there was such an obvious love for the people of that great nation, China. When your love in other people's hearts made it possible for me to take that trip there last spring, I felt the same thing! I loved those upturned faces that peered into the windows of our bus. We were greeted with friendly smiles everywhere we went. And I loved the beautiful little children in the nursery school and in the primary school we visited. They clapped their hands to welcome us and sang some of their songs. You made every one of them; you love every one. And ought not we learn some things from them?

How remarkable it was that my peer roommate (both of us 78 years old) and I could go out at night into the big cities and be unafraid. More than that, how wonderful to have the joy of young people gathering around us, practicing their English—young people with friendly faces and shiny eyes. And we marveled that we did not have to lock the door of our hotel room, and we never needed nor were permitted to pay any tips. And from information gathered and from what we saw, there was no

longer mass starvation; there were very few obese people, but apparently the food was better distributed, and there was enough for life. Surely, God, this is pleasing to you, isn't it?

The shops were filled with people and filled with things to buy! I'm sure that all is not utopia, and there were those awful 10 years when countless were killed, when all the schools were closed, when tyranny, godlessness, and destruction were rampant. But now it seems there's a glimmer of hope for a new age. I believe history is going somewhere. I dare believe that, because of your coming to earth in the person of your Son, and the life, death, and resurrection of Jesus—and his coming again—we can look forward to the great promise of what is to come. I believe that this church of China, in a land that numbers one-fourth of the world's population, is standing at the door of an unprecedented opportunity to break some of the old patterns that bound us—with the empowering of the Holy Spirit and the support of our prayers.

They can lead the world to a new era where the Isaiah proclamation Jesus quoted at the synagogue in Nazareth could become the Magna Charta: "The Spirit of the Lord is upon me, Because he anointed me to preach good tidings to the poor: He hath sent me to proclaim release to the captives, And recovering of sight to the blind, To set at liberty them that are bruised, To proclaim the acceptable year of the Lord" (Luke 4:18-19 Phillips).

I want to follow you down that path, God. It

was thrilling to stand in a classroom at the seminary newly reopened in Nankin and read on the chalkboard in Greek, Chinese, and English your words, "I am the light of the world. The man who follows me will never walk in the dark but will live his life in light" (John 8:12 Phillips). I'll never forget how our Chinese guide leaned over to read it. He apparently was unfamiliar with Scripture; he had had no direct contact with the message of Christ. Yet he was so accommodating about making arrangements for us to attend a church service, to visit this seminary, to meet people with whom some of our party had connections. And he was so thoughtful about our comfort and health. We learned to love that man, and now even a year later, he is often in my prayers! Please, God, bless Mr. Yi with your presence.

I'm full of things to say about your great, wide world, Lord. Will you bear with me some more? Even as I write that line, in my heart I see the smile of your Spirit. I'm believing that you understand my enthusiasm! Thank you, God of love!

Ruth

13

Dear God,

When I finished that last letter, it seemed to me I had just begun to tell you about my China visit. When I told you about our guide, I was struck with the electric question: What witness to you did our relationship with him give? Could he sense the joy of your presence in us? And even more, did we evidence your love for all people, your concern about injustice, hatred, and killing? It's a very sobering question.

I remember hearing about a person in the Middle East who found that Christian work among the Muslim could be very frustrating, yet patiently and lovingly she lived your presence among them. One day a stranger inquired of a Muslim teacher if he knew the whereabouts of this woman. The teacher's reply was, "Oh, do you mean the lady who wears on her the presence of the prophet Jesus and rubs him off on everyone she meets?" And I remember my "girls" in the Occoquan prison singing as they left our Bible study, "Let the beauty of Jesus be seen in me!"

I want to thank you for that Easter service you made possible in Xian! On the Thursday evening before, we had had our own little "upper room" experience in a hotel room that was granted to us. I know it was your Spirit that provided that! It was something to remember! Jonathan Lindell, our resource person, had poured out his heart in a message from your Word. We were reminded of why we were gathered—"This do in remembrance of me"—and then in faith we were cleansed from the sins we had confessed. A Presbyterian minister who had been a missionary in India served the elements. They were different! We used what was available: orange pop and a Chinese biscuit. But they became the vehicle of your presence as in faith we received them. You didn't mind about the awkward symbols, did you, Lord? I shall always remember the holy moments in that upper room.

As Easter Sunday approached, our leader asked our guide if it would be possible to attend a Christian service on that special day. You must have been working in his heart because later he announced he had made arrangements for us to go to the Sunday evening service. As you well know, this church had been quite recently reopened under the new three-point program specified by the now more liberal government: 1) The church must be Chinese, administered and run by the Chinese; 2) it must be the Chinese *Christian* church, no denominations; 3) it must be supported by the Chinese with no outside help, except the reunification with the Church of Taiwan. What do you think about this, Lord?

The service we attended was the third one held in that church that Easter Sunday, and all had been packed! What an experience!

You were there! As we walked down the aisle (37 of us) to the reserved places in the front, hands would reach out from the pews as a gesture of friendship. And what a moment as the choir rose to sing, "Christ the Lord Is Risen Today, Alleluia"! We joined them in our language, and the Chinese and the English were blended together in one great victorious paean of praise! Jonathan reported to us afterward (he could understand the language of the pastor) that the sermon was a strong, gospel presentation of your resurrection. Afterwards, when the congregation was dismissed, we remained with the choir and had a thrilling conclusion of the fellowship of faith as we joined, they in their tongue, and we in ours, in the hymn, "What a Friend We Have in Jesus." We were all together, Lord, all barriers removed, with you, our resurrected Savior, at the center. Thank you!

Ruth

14

Dear God,

Before I leave my thoughts about China, there are some other things I want to mention, and telling you helps me to remember. It was astonishing for us to hear that the Christian church actually grew in membership during those years of depression. We were told there are many more Christians today in China than there were before the revolution.

Maybe first of all, we should take a look at what caused the revolution! The wealthy ruling class had made literal slaves of the poor peasants. Millions were starving, and despair became such a way of life for them that there seemed to be no way out. I know this isn't the way you want things to be! Then there was engendered a spark of hope and the grass fires spread until the nation was consumed.

I don't have to tell you, Lord, how horrible the process was! Death, destruction, deceit, and indescribable deviltry were a part of the revolution. It was a bitter price to pay, but at this point there has emerged a somewhat classless society, where everybody's contribution is considered of equal value. What do you think of this, Lord? What is your pattern for living?

Just today in our devotions we were reminded that when we appear before your throne, there will be no preferential status, that there are no degrees of sinning, that all have fallen short, that the ground before the cross is level, and that your saving grace is for all!

Again and again you remind us in your Word to have concern for the poor, for judgment will fall on those who oppress them! You remind us that all the gifts of the earth are yours, not for a few to consume, but for all to have enough to live. Don't we need an overhaul of our economic system? I think you'd better begin with me. I really don't need a two-bedroom apartment. Help me decisively to act on this awareness now! Keep me from rationalizing out of it!

But to get back to China, it was thrilling to learn at the seminary in Nankin that when they sent out word that they could offer Bible study courses by mail, the response was overwhelming! Thousands requested them!

It seems that during the years of religious persecution, the church found its sanctuary in the family circle. The family tradition is very strong in China, and not even the despotic government could break this. So where there were Christian people, the family became the nucleus of fellowship, and, often surreptitiously, neighbors would join. We are told in China today there are thousands of such Christian cells. It is the leaders of these who are now responding to the opportunity of continued learning that the seminary is offering.

How wonderful you are, God! You take failure and use it for a blessing; you take obstacles and make them stepping-stones! You do it for us individually and you do it for us collectively.

In my life, you have used the difficult times for growth and strengthening of faith. They are the times when you have been the closest.

Lord, the belligerent, bungling, bleeding world needs you so desperately! Make me a channel of healing!

Ruth

15

Dear God,

How much fun it has been sharing memories with my family here in Bernhausen, in West Germany. When we're gathered about the table, Inge and Karl prime the pump of the past. It doesn't take much priming for me to get going.

But the other day, we had a glimpse of boyhood memories from one of the guests. We had been talking about how Hitler had mesmerized the people so they didn't know what was going on: the death trains to Auschwitz, the inferno of Dachau, the elimination from society of the mentally ill and the aged and the sick. When we were protesting the Trident's entrance into the waters of the West Coast, the archbishop of Seattle called this monster submarine of death "the Auschwitz of Puget Sound." We protestors were determined to do everything in our power, nonviolently, to hinder its path, even if it meant giving our lives.

This friend, then, told us of a memory that haunted him. He said he was 10 years old when he became a part of the "Hitler Youth"! It was the patriotic thing to do, and all his buddies were in it. The leader trained them with great precision to march in step and to properly salute, and to obey the *Führer!* He remembered that one day the old Catholic priest was coming out of the church as this sizable group of boys under the leader came marching down the street.

The priest, he said, was so old that even in the altar ring he had to hold onto the rail when he turned because his feet were so uncertain. He was really very frail.

From the church, he slowly stepped out into the street. His steps were short and his progress slow, so before he could reach the other side, the marching boys were upon him. Then, he said, their leader ordered the boys to surround the priest and imprison him in their circle, where they belittled him and poked fun at him. Our friend said that he knew he should have broken away and refused to become a part of such sadistic cruelty, of such utter disrespect for age. But he wasn't strong enough; he feared what his peers as well as his leader would say.

He never told us what became of the priest, but he said that all through the years he has been haunted by that memory. And sadly enough, his life reflects it. He has not been able to find himself, in spite of the musical gifts with which you have endowed him. He needs you to heal his memories, and it is only you who can do it.

As we bring to you our ugly remembrances, the times we've been cowardly and thoughtless, and ask your forgiveness, you give us the promise of forgiving and remembering no more. I plead for that, Lord, for the people I know who are haunted by the ghosts of past mistakes and lost opportunities.

Help us all to take each day as a new beginning and not let the devil immobilize with unforgiven remorse!

Your presence in us is victorious over the past, present, and future. So empower us to live victoriously! Thank you! Thank you again!

Ruth

16

Dear God,

Help, Lord, help! I feel like a drowning child in a turbulent sea. I want to swim and help others around me who are drowning. But the waves are high and powerful, and I can hardly keep myself afloat! In your book there is recorded a similar cry from one of your children: "From the depths of my despair I call to you, Lord. Hear my cry, O Lord; listen to my call for help!" (Ps. 130:1-2 TEV).

My burden is a part of the news report I heard on the radio yesterday. I couldn't believe my ears. The report was that there was a Pentagon paper found telling of a five-year nuclear war plan in which we, of course, would come out on top. God, where are you, that in my country, which likes to call itself Christian, such a thing could be born? This really means planned destruction of your world—the decimation of grain fields and forests, the polluting of rivers and oceans, infecting humans with cancer and concomitant diseases even if they have survived the blast! I want to beat my fists against somebody's door and say, "No! No! This must not be!"

And now they are calling the MX missile "the Peacekeeper"! Lord, that's sacrilege! It's blasphemy! It's a part of the same pattern of the "christening"

that was reported the other day: the warhead-equipped submarine that was named *City of Corpus Christi!* I shudder!

I've written to you before about this. What can I do? Do I just sit by? I hear young people say, "What's the use? The world is going to be all blown up! What's the use of our planning or studying?" On the one hand that's the way I feel, but on the other hand I believe there is still time for the course to change! It may be four minutes to twelve—but you can work miracles in four minutes. You can work miracles in the twinkling of an eye. All right, God! Use me! Show me what you want me to do.

I guess I'd better confess my prayer life hasn't been what it should be. The fuel of faith too often has been lacking. I've wanted to superimpose my will for yours! And, Lord, I've been so remiss in love, especially toward those who don't agree with me. I get impatient and hateful. Lord, cleanse me of the debris of ill will and antagonism that clutters the channel through which your love can flow. Then, by your grace, fill me with thoughts and words and deeds of compassion and concern. Help me to begin with those around me and to reach out to the ends of the earth. Use my pen, my voice, and my voting, Lord, as your instruments. Let me be a bearer of hope in spite of Pentagon leaks and radio reports.

Hear the cry of this grandmother, Lord. Hear her cry not only for her grandchildren but for all the children of the world. Restore us to sanity, to putting our faith in you, to being instruments of your peace.

Out of the depths I cry, O Lord! Hear my prayer!

Ruth

— 17 —

Dear God,

You've done it again! The cry in my last letter found a spark of hope in a copy of *Stars and Stripes* I saw as I came down to join the family after my writing. On the front page was an article with a huge headline about the very things I had written: "D.O.D. Study Ponders Long A-War"! There were the details of the plans that had so shaken me.

Then I turned to the second page—and there it was—something of your answer in just as big a headline: "Religious Leaders Urge A-ban"! The opening paragraph gave me hope: "Religious leaders representing millions of churchgoers around the world called for a banning of nuclear arms and said there is no cause that can morally justify atomic warfare. . . ." It told about a declaration by leading

Soviet bloc and Western scientists that condemned nuclear arms and the arms race. Then there was this line by one of the church leaders: "This is how we can help—by raising our public voices!"

So, God, that's how I'll try to become a part of the answer. But as I am quiet before you, I think I hear you saying something more: "Don't just be *against* something; be *for* what I am—*love!*"

That word is bandied about so lightly. But what meaning it has when it embodies all you are! Caring Creator, suffering Servant, crucified Christ, strengthening Spirit! In your power, help us to launch a great offensive of love! What a new frontier to be a part of! What a reason for living!

Best of all, Lord, I can begin right where I am with those with whom I live, those I meet on the street, in the shops wherever I go. With your help, I can see people out of the eyes of love; I can think loving thoughts about them. Through prayer I can fly love around the world.

To some people this will sound very foolish and naive. But you have spoken of this, too, in your Word: "that things may be hidden from the wise, and revealed unto babes." And to these people, you say, "Try me and see." That's a pretty scientific way.

In my last letter, I was so discouraged, but now I have a new infusion of hope. You *are* working in the hearts of people everywhere. There comes to mind those beautiful lines your servant recorded in the letter to the Corinthians so many years ago (they mean just as much today): "Thanks be to God who leads us, wherever we are, on Christ's triumphant way and makes our knowledge of him spread throughout the world like a lovely perfume! We Christians have the unmistakable 'scent' of Christ, discernible alike to those who are being saved and to those who are heading for death. To the latter it seems like the deathly smell of doom, to the former it has the refreshing fragrance of life itself" (2 Cor. 2:14-16 Phillips).

Count me in, Lord!

Ruth

------------------ 18 ------------------

Dear God,

It seems as if I come to you only with problems. I thank and praise you that you never turn me away! But I believe the things that are bothering me are bothering you, too! This time it's the matter of all the refugees, Lord, and how to help them. I have a feeling you have a very tender heart for these people, because you told us how "the foxes have holes; and the birds have nests, but you had no place

to lay your head." And like you, Lord, there are many millions of people today who have been forced to leave their homes. By the political turmoil and fighting that ensued, by the destruction of even their simplest dwellings, by the burning of their land, often making it untillable—they had to leave. Surely, Lord, this isn't the kind of world you planned!

You know how many countries are closing their doors to these homeless people. It's not easy for these refugees. Jobs are scarce, they don't know the language, and often they're separated from their families. But you do want us to be concerned and help them, don't you? And you've warned us not to grow weary in well doing! And you have blessed those people and churches that have stuck in there and shared their hearts and their homes. And we need to keep doing this. In a home I know, they flavor the world as folks from Vietnam, Eritrea, Central America, and Indonesia find refuge there. But, Lord, don't we need to get at the source of the problem?

I remember hearing the story of a man who, while fishing in a stream, suddenly saw someone in the water calling for help. He dived in and dragged the man to shore; then he looked up and saw another frantically yelling to him. So he went in after him, too. And just as he pulled the second man out, a person passed by and said: "Don't you think you'd better go to the bridge and see who is pushing them in?" I'm sure that's what you want us to do: ask what the cause is of all these homeless people. Yes, what is it, Lord?

Is it our greed—those of us who have so much, and the millions who don't have nearly enough? Is it lust for power—the desire to rule and conquer others—that makes people flee? Lord, help us to get at the root of it! Help those who know you to be willing to live with less, to love more, to follow you. We need to see you in every homeless person, to hear you say to us, "I was lonely and you made me welcome" (Matt. 25:35 Phillips). And while we're doing that in the places where we live, we need to be responsible Christian citizens urging our government to become part of the solution by helping needy countries not to wage war and buy arms but to develop agricultural needs and their own resources. It's only your Spirit, Lord, that can do this.

Fill us with your Holy Spirit! Give us wisdom and imagination and daring and courage in solving these world problems. Help us to begin where we are!

Ruth

19

Dear God,

In yesterday's letter, as I talked to you about the refugees, I was reminded of the many people who are really trying to help. I want to be thankful for them, Lord. Your love shines right through them. I remember how you used the dispersion of the Jews as a means of spreading your message to the then-known world. Surely you are giving us a special opportunity in the countless number of people from distant places who come to our shores.

But please, God, help us not to make their becoming Christian a condition for our giving help! That's what we call "bread and butter" Christians. Let your love in us be so strong and sure that we reach out to anyone in need and leave the results to you. May the graces of your presence—compassion, gentleness, kindness, understanding, trust—be the witness of your place in our lives. And help us to respect all people, to learn from them, and to treat them as equals. Forgive us for wanting credit for what we do! Sometimes the statistics in our church reports make me want to vomit! They seem to say, "Look how good we are!" Deliver us, Lord, from such pride!

Lines from many hymns come to my mind when I think about pride! I think it's the number one sin. That's what Archbishop Temple told the people of England. He said all sin could be summed up in one letter: "I"!

How well I remember my beloved mother beginning her prayers with:

> Just as I am, without one plea,
> But that thy blood was shed for me,
> And that thou bidd'st me come to thee,
> O Lamb of God, I come. I come.

And from "Rock of Ages" the lines:

> Nothing in my hand I bring;
> Simply to thy cross I cling.
> Naked, come to thee for dress;
> Helpless, look to thee for grace.

This morning, Lord, I would ask you to search out my heart, and cleanse it from any vestige of pride! Search out my motives for my giving, my visiting, yes, even my concern! And do it every day!

Thank you for your forgiving, inclusive, everlasting love!

Ruth

20

Dear God,

Today I was thinking about the many different people who have crossed my path and how each of them have left something of themselves. I guess that's what the poet meant when he said: "I am a part of all that I have met."

When I was talking to you about refugees, I thought about the Remer family that came to us in Washington, D.C. They were from Poland, and in those days we called them "DP's," meaning displaced persons. There were six in all: father, mother, twin boys, another boy, and a girl. They lived in our parsonage for some time while we tried to find a house for them. They couldn't speak a word of

English, so we had an interesting experience using our hands and eyes.

I remember sitting down at the piano one day and playing some hymns. Mrs. Remer came into the room with her eyes just shining as she hummed with the piano the melody to "Praise to the Lord, the Almighty, the King of Creation." Music had bridged the chasm of language, and we were one in the Spirit as we joined in that song. That's the miracle of your presence, Lord!

And in what unsuspecting places it reveals itself! Our folks in Bernhausen have given refuge to countless people! I was visiting with them when we celebrated the joy of an Eritrean father being re-united with his Russian wife and child. They lived with our family for some time. One day the woman was breaking bread and our daughter noticed that when she had kneaded it well and was about to set

it aside to rise, she made a cross with her fingers in the dough. When Biz inquired about it, she told of how her mother always did that to acknowledge that the bread was a gift from you! And you said of yourself: "I am the bread of life."

This made me think about the amazing variety of breads there is throughout the world. In Ulm, West Germany, we visited a bread museum. It showed all the different kinds of bread through all the different ages. What a display of shapes, tastes, and textures! In every age there was variation due to the kinds of ovens and materials that were available. And yet in each were the basics that make each loaf the staff of life.

What a symbol that is, Lord, of how you come to each one of us. You meet us where we are, all of us with our own personalities and backgrounds, our own tastes and preferences. And no matter how the outward form may vary, the essence, the life-giving nourishment is the same.

Thank you for not making us like so many peas in a pod. Thank you for the wonder and variety of your creation! Thank you that your presence in the world can bring unity in diversity.

Lord, you are the answer!

Ruth

21

Dear God,

I've seen you several times these last days, sometimes in the most unsuspecting places and sometimes just the evidence that you have been there—kind of like your footprints!

Without her really knowing about it, I think it was your Spirit in our Russian friend that caused her to send a special little Christmas gift over to each one of us. She is the one who told about her mother putting a cross in the bread dough.

And the other morning when I came down to breakfast, I knew you had been there in the spirit of my granddaughter, who, before she went to school, left a little note on my plate and on her mother's. Mine read, "I love you, Grandma, very much." And surely it was you who accompanied her to school and caused her to come home so jubilantly with an A on her chemistry test. Not that she hadn't studied!

Yes, and you must have been the one that caused Karl, our grandson, after he had just finished his *Abitur,* three days of entrance exams, to say to me, "Grandma, would it help if I typed your letters for you?"

When it snowed the other night, and the menfolk had gone, Walle to Stuttgart for his work, and

Karl to school, I saw you in Biz, shoveling off the walk of the lonely old widow across the street.

It was you in the heart of that young Indonesian pastor that prompted him to leave his family in Munich and come to Stuttgart to help the wife and family of his friend who was having an operation.

I saw you in those spectacular amaryllis, that breathtaking bouquet that Biz's friend sent to visibly bring your presence into this home; I see you in that blooming cactus that is outdoing itself by blooming twice in the matter of a few months, and

in those pansy faces that are peeking through the snow.

I heard you last night, Lord, in that glorious concert in the *Stifts Kirche,* when soloists, choir, and instruments combined to interpret the gifts of music you had given to Bach, Mozart, and Beethoven. You were in the fluid, soaring notes of that soprano as she sang your praise.

I heard you in your Word this morning as I read about the daring of your apostles as they witnessed to your life and resurrection even though they were threatened with imprisonment; I heard you and was ashamed at my own cowardice and lack of courage!

You were in the sensitive kindness of that young man who changed his plans for the evening to accompany that weird and bewildered older man to dinner and to make the occasion a happy one.

How many times do I miss your footprints in the course of a day? I'm so quick to see the wrong and the ugly in people. Please open my eyes to your presence in everyone I meet. And work a miracle again, Lord! Let people see you in me!

Ruth

22

Dear God,

Here in Germany they've been asking me to share something of my experience at Puget Sound last August. The magnitude of that experience, the influence of it on my life is hard to put into words.

You know, Lord, that public demonstrations and protests have not exactly been my line. When David marched in Selma on behalf of civil rights, I certainly encouraged him. And I admired greatly the many who fronted that battle in a beautiful, nonviolent way. Oh, yes, and I remember now, I marched with 30,000 others in Chicago with Martin Luther King protesting the exclusive real estate zoning. We marched from Soldier's Field to Mayor Daley's office. We marched shoulder to shoulder with our black friends, singing, "We shall overcome!" That was a great experience even though there were folks on the curbing spitting at us and saying evil things! But we didn't disobey the law.

This summer was different! When I read Robert Aldrich's book *Counter Force Syndrome* and Dr. Helen Caldicott's *Nuclear Madness*, I knew I had to do everything in my power to protest the nuclear proliferation; I felt your Spirit giving me courage and opening the way. I was challenged by the example of Aldrich who, with a large family to support, gave up his job as a chief engineer at the Bangor base where the Trident was to be armed. When he realized they were preparing a first strike weapon, he felt in conscience he could no longer be a part of it. I marvel, Lord, how you use different people from a variety of places.

Next Jon gave me the book *The Hundreth Monkey* and that, coupled with Caldicott's book, made me realize each person did count, and one person could be the turning point. So, when Jon said he was going to be in the flotilla of small boats protesting the Trident missile submarine's entrance into Puget Sound, I told him I wanted to be with him. As I look back on it all, Lord, I see your amazing guidance each step of the way.

Biz left her family in Chicago to accompany me to Seattle for the advent of the Trident. That was an experience all of its own. We were among more than 40 people gathered not far from the place from which this monster was supposed to come. We slept and ate and were schooled in "yurts"—about 20 to 30 in each! The sleeping facilities were the ground and sleeping bags. I had a special accommodation with a wooden bench for my bed. There was no running water, and sanitation facilities were through the blackberry patch up the hill a ways. Food amazingly was provided by people from a neighboring town. These were the crudest camping provisions I had ever experienced. And yet there was such an absorption in what we were about to

do, such a dedication and earnestness in learning what care to take if we were plunged into the cold water and how to fend off attacks from fellow prisoners if we were incarcerated and, more particularly, how to be not only nonviolent in our protest, but to be armed with love.

It rained most of the time. We were very crowded, and sleep was at a minimum. And yet there was an exhilaration for which there are no words. There was work to do, a witness to be given that our strength as a nation should not be in weapons to destroy the earth, but in trusting in you as we learn to share the resources of your wonderful creation with all the world.

Your Word had our sending orders; it was our resource book. Your presence was our empowering. Thank you, Lord of life and love, for your guidance!

Ruth

23

Dear God,

Bear with me, but I must get the rest of the Trident story written, partly because it was one of the most significant experiences of my life, and again because you were so much a part of it. You were so really there.

You know how the plan had been to string little rowboats across the path of the Trident, this monster of the sea, two football fields long and four stories high. Nor is it just its size or cost. There are two other counts against it: it carries 408 warheads, each four or five times more powerful than the one dropped at Hiroshima (which means it represents 2040 Hiroshimas), and it is a first strike weapon. I'll bet you were smiling at that fantastic dream of your children at Ground Zero, that a flotilla of little boats could even for one minute deter that powerful monster. We didn't stop it, Lord, but we surely delayed it!

You must have provided those two big sailboats that became pilot boats. Wasn't it wonderful the way they represented the world: The *Pacific Peacemaker* from Australia, and the *Lizard of Woz* from Canada? Each had a crew of about 10 or 12 and each had little rowboats attached to it by heavy rope. The *Lizard* had nine little lizards; the *Peacemaker* had ten ducklings. In the little lizards there was room for only one person; in the ducklings there could be one rower and one person. Then we had three boats with outboard motors, to be emergency boats as needed. Jon's was christened the S.S. *Plowshares*, and our theme song was:

> Then everyone 'neath the vine and fig trees,
> Shall live at peace and unafraid.
> And into plowshares beat their swords;
> Nations shall learn war no more.

We came to love those words from your book.

The five of us in our boat represented a variety of occupations and ages: a young college professor, a university chaplain, a doctor's wife and nurse administrator, a deaconess who worked with the poor, and this old lady. In each of us you were the moving Spirit, Lord.

You know how the Quaker lookout people reported to us when the Trident went through the Panama Canal so we could know about when to expect it. For seven days we were out on that large body of water at five o'clock in the morning and stayed out until six at night waiting expectantly. There were some beautiful moments when the porpoises put on spectacular performances for us or when schools of little silver fish made beautiful patterns close to the water's surface. There were some not-so-spectacular moments when the rain drizzled and the wind blew and, in spite of long, woolen underwear and sweaters and rain capes, we were wet and cold. But you took care of us. You were there all the time. And it was special when Archbishop Hunthausen, and the bishops and clergy from the Washington Council of Churches, and the rabbi, came out in a witness boat to have prayers and support us. That was just the day before the *event!* Everybody felt that next day had to be the day!

And it was! Already by five in the morning the Coast Guard boats began zooming in, before either the *Lizard* or *Peacemaker* could pull anchor. And though they were in legitimate water, they were surrounded and boarded and waterhosed and impounded. The ropes to the little boats were cut— and row as some of their occupants did, they could make little headway on their own "steam" toward the Trident. Biz was rowing one of these little boats with Sister Jean sitting straight and supportive in the other seat. They tried, frail crafts that they were, many with women at the oars. My last thought as I saw them bobbing in the swirling waters was of helpless, little children on the sea of life. Yet, in another sense, they were more powerful than the Trident itself. Their empowering was love! You know about that because that's what you are—love incarnate!

I love you!

Ruth

24

Dear God,

This letter should be the end of my Trident story! But there's so much to tell and if I write it I'll remember it better. Please help me to recall it accurately, Lord.

When Jon saw that the beautiful plan of stringing the little boats in front of the path of the Trident had been stopped, he made a break from the *Peacemaker* and we zoomed out in the direction of the Trident. It was quite a scene that we left: helicopters overhead—maybe a dozen of them from the Navy and the news media—and the 99 Coast Guard boats that had been commandeered to thwart our plans. We learned later how the water guns were used so that some of the crew were washed overboard; how, when one of the nuns held up a loaf of bread, she was water-gunned down; how, when the skipper of the *Lizard* refused to leave his post, they water-gunned him off and then he was arrested because his boat hit a Coast Guard boat. The folks on both the big boats were handcuffed and told to sit on the floor. That was the scene we left. To begin with we were unnoticed. Then a Coast Guard boat spotted us and began hailing us to stop. We had agreed that we would try to get over the line the government had set as prohibitive. It was a little amusing how they kept ex-

tending it, so the new orders had to be read to us each time. We kept barreling along, even though the penalty had also increased. Now crossing the line was a felony with a probable $10,000 fine and 10 years in prison. That was really something to contemplate, Lord, but we knew you would be with us, so we weren't afraid. Now two other boats had joined in pursuit of us. Three different times we were stopped with the offer to turn back. Each time we joined hands, prayed the prayer you taught us, then pressed on again. We finally knew we had crossed the line, so then we stopped. At one of the stops, we almost got water-gunned. When I saw the young man pull the hose out I called to him, "No! No! You can't do that in my America!" And bless him, he put the hose back in!

Well, the rest was routine. We were handcuffed and transferred to a large Navy prison boat close by. After being fingerprinted and photographed we were sent down to the "brig" where we remained handcuffed and behind the bars, with an armed guard sitting outside the door. Three other protesters who were arrested joined us. Then the boat moved down Hood Canal to Bangor where the Trident was housed. We were taken off the boat and transferred by bus to a barbed wire enclosure. You know how funny it was, Lord, that the Navy had provided 12 "Sani-cans" for us. We were finally 14 prisoners in all, which meant there was almost one a piece. But they were the only places to sit! We must have spent four hours there—a good time for communicating with you. Then they put us into buses with guards, and in another couple of hours we were at the courthouse in Seattle where a huge crowd awaited our arrival. Dave and Mary had come from Chicago to be our "support" people, and they now had been reunited with Biz. They had not known where we were all day. Some beautiful signs greeted us: "Bless You, Plowshares" and "Peace on Earth."

We were hustled into the courthouse to appear before a fine judge who released all of us on recognizance (including the two international skippers) with the promise we would return August 30 for our arraignment.

When we came out of the courthouse, we were greeted with love—and the media. One little girl ran up and hugged me. That was precious, Lord! When the TV reporter asked me whether I thought it was wrong to disobey the laws of my country, I said an emphatic: "No! I did it for the children of the world."

You had helped me settle that question when in your book I read what Peter said: "We must obey God rather than men" (Acts 5:29). I knew that making such horrible instruments of death could never be your will; nor would you want my country to break the treaties it had made. I was obeying your higher law!

I slept like a baby that night with a heart overflowing with gratitude to you!

Ruth

25

Dear God,

Today I need to bare my aching heart! Where shall I begin?

This family has taken into the circle of its home a young Eritrean man who is in political asylum from his country. He was only 16 years old when he had to flee. His offense was handing out in school leaflets critical of the government. Of course his two older brothers had been critical of the government before.

Through a compassionate doctor's wife in this little city, he has been enrolled in a high school a couple of hours from here. For vacation time and free weekends, this is his home; he is a part of this loving family. But his visa and passport status is so uncertain. People are objecting to too many refugees coming in. He thought it was all settled, then his lawyer called and said an appeal was being made to rescind the decision for him and 30 others. So he's in limbo; he doesn't know what will happen! All the while he's trying to work hard in school, learn a new language, and keep up with his studies. But some of his schoolmates ridicule him and resent him.

You know how we turned to you in prayer yesterday morning, as we always do. We were going to your house. Biz was leading us. You know the burden in her heart, in all our hearts—the threat of nuclear extinction, the hatred and dissension everywhere, the uncertainties! Then from across the table came some of the most violent sobs I have ever heard. Remember how in my heart I cried out to you to help this young man? Were you talking to him when he went up to his room? You must have been, because after a while his sobs subsided. Then Biz and Walle went up to talk to him and he told them he was worried about what would happen. They became a part of your answer to help in any way they could. But when he had to leave in the afternoon to return to school, he seemed so sad and alone. Our hearts ached for him!

Lord, surround him with your love. Help him to turn to you! Assuage his loneliness with your presence. Raise up for him a special friend at school. And put it upon the heart of the authorities to clear his status. Show us what we can do!

That was the first heartache! Then last night there came a telephone call from the U.S. about another situation. It's so complicated; you've got to help.

Some years ago, a Chinese friend had to flee the mainland and go to Taiwan. He had to leave his wife and four children. While he was trying to make arrangements for them to join him, he received a letter from his wife saying their relationship was all over. Of course he was very sad, but during the years that passed he met a young widow with a little baby girl. He obtained a divorce on the grounds of desertion and married the widow. She was a lovely person and made him a good wife. Two children were born to that union; yet he loved the widow's little girl just as much. Now these children are pretty much grown up. The family has prospered. For a good part of the time both the husband and wife had gainful jobs outside the home.

Then came the blow. Now that relationships have eased with the mainland, his first family has made contact with him and wants help for the children's higher education. The second wife feels that a terrible wedge has come between them. They are not talking to each other. The older girl from Taiwan (now a young woman) is heartbroken at her stepfather's attitude. There had been a beautiful relationship between them before.

Lord, only you can untie that knotty problem. Help them all to turn to you for the solution. Break down the barriers so that they'll communicate with each other.

Once I read a sign in a shop: "We mend everything but broken hearts!" I believe broken hearts are your specialty and nothing is too hard for you.

I bring these beloved friends to you! Help, Lord, please!

Ruth

26

Dear God,

There are so many things I don't understand, so many things in your book, especially in the Old Testament. What do you mean in your book when you say: "I have loved Jacob and his descendants, and have hated Esau and his descendants" (Mal. 1:2-3, also Rom. 9:13 TEV)? I've just been reading about the horrible revenge Jacob's sons took on Shechem and his people for what he had done to their sister, Dinah. First they completely broke their word, then they slaughtered, plundered, and enslaved. I know, Lord, that such action is entirely against your nature and will. How grateful I am that you revealed your nature in ways I can understand, in the person of your Son, Jesus Christ. I am so grateful for the description of your Son in Hebrews 1:2-4: "Through the Son God made the whole universe, and to the Son he has ordained that all creation should ultimately belong. This Son, radiance of the glory of God, flawless expression of the nature of God, himself the upholding principle of all that is" (Phillips). I rest my faith in that revelation. What a pattern to follow!

But we can so glibly quote parts of your book and justify most anything we do. I am burdened by the way our president quotes the Bible. The radio gave a report of his speech to the religious broadcasters. He said that if we followed the Ten Commandments and the Golden Rule, all would be well. Does he do that? Is he challenging us to "Love our enemies," to "do good to those who hate us," to "if our enemy hunger, feed him," to "go the second mile," to "turn the other cheek," and most particularly, as a nation, to put our trust in you and not in the "chariots" of war; to put aside the sword; to make a priority of the cause of the poor and those who suffer injustice? Lord, how can we get through to him and our other leaders that putting their trust in nuclear weapons is worshiping a false god?

When I was a young girl, there was an old song: "Praise the Lord, and Pass the Ammunition." That seems to be the theme song of what we are doing as a nation. Lord, deliver us from such perfidy before it is too late! Raise up leaders who will truly put their trust in you!

And thank you for all those who are risking their lives on behalf of peace. Thank you for the growing number who are even in jail because of nonviolent civil disobedience: action that speaks louder than words. Thank you for the way they make their prison experience a living prayer, a witness to your sustaining grace as they seek to follow your will.

Yes, thank you, Lord, for those who baked and distributed bread to the nuclear workers as they left their jobs—distributed it as a symbol of what the hungry of the world need—bread instead of bombs!

Thank you for those three nuns who undoubtedly will be arrested and incarcerated for their walking the tracks into the base—the tracks on which trains filled with deadly nuclear weapons will travel. Thank you for those women who walked the tracks in love for all involved.

Thank you for those leaders in the church who

are daring to speak out against this false god of power.

Forgive us, Lord, for our cowardice, our lack of faith.

One of your loving children, Dr. Kagawa, prayed a prayer that finds its echo in my heart. He was praying for his country, Japan. I pray it for my beloved country, America!

> Lord, not for self alone
> Thus do I groan.
> My nation's burdens are the load I bear.
> O Lord, hear my prayer!
> Strike off the chains that bind
> My well-loved land!

Before it is too late, Lord!

Ruth

27

Dear God,

Forgive me that so many of my letters are complaints and criticism and questions and problems. If all the people who turn to you follow my pattern, you must be terribly weary of us all! There I go again, making your image like ours. Now I recall that we are told that Jesus was in all things like us, except he was without sin! That's a very big "except"! And in your Word I find a confirming witness to this matter of your never growing weary: "Don't you know? Haven't you heard? The Lord is the everlasting God; he created all the world. He never grows tired or weary" (Isa. 40:28 TEV). Thank you for the comfort and hope that gives me!

But today I want to take a look at my blessings and write my thank you to you. You are the author and finisher of everything that is good!

Thank you for my parents! I don't have to tell you that you were first in their love in relationship to those around them. Thank you for a father who didn't give much show of affection outwardly (like hugging and kissing) but who was a "Rock of Gibraltar" whenever we needed him. Thank you for a mother who was loads of fun and generous and compassionate! In the most serious manner she would say to a friend, putting her hand on the friend's shoulder: "You know, there is one thing I have against you!" Then, when in consternation the friend would ask, "What is that?" she would laughingly respond, "My hand!" Thank you for her sense of humor.

Thank you for my childhood and the sisters and brothers who helped to make our home such a good place.

Thank you for the church—its pastor and church school teachers who strengthened what I learned about you in my home, who provided the joy of Christian fellowship. Thank you for the opportunity of learning, the schools my country provided.

Thank you for my country, where I'm free to search for the truth and speak out against the things that are wrong.

Thank you for a beloved husband, with whom it was such fun to live and with whom I was a privileged partner in so many exciting projects and places.

Thank you for our children, each of whom has not only brought joy but has challenged us to understand the larger world and to grow in a greater concept of your love. Thank you for our grandchildren, all 19 of them, each so different and each as precious.

Thank you for countless friends, prayer partners, and concerned Christians who with their love have enriched our lives!

Thank you for your beautiful world, for trees and desert, for mountains and valleys, for lakes and rivers, for rain and sunshine, for the changing seasons. Thank you for the beauty of flowers and weeds, of a storm-swept sky and a placid blue one, of a starlit sky with a fingernail of a moon suggesting there's more to come. Thank you for sunsets firing windows and lakes and giving a little foretaste of the glory beyond!

Lord, I've only begun!

> What language shall I borrow
> To thank you, dearest friend,
> For this your dying sorrow,
> Your pity without end?
>
> O make me yours forever,
> And should I fainting be,
> Lord, let me never, never
> Outlive my love for thee!

Ruth

28

Dear God,

There are some questions I've been wanting to ask you, and one in particular, after reading a book written by a pastor. This question has come up several times before, but because I know personally the man who wrote the book, it hit me with particular force. It's the matter of the baptism of the Holy Spirit and the speaking in tongues.

I've read and reread that Chapter 14 of 1 Corinthians and then that magnificent Chapter 13 on love! We're told about how you have given a variety of gifts to us, none of them independent of the others, but each needing the others. And when the gift of tongues is mentioned, you say it's a good gift, but that it's better to witness to you in words people understand than in a strange language, unless there is an interpreter. Yet those who have been given the "tongue gift" often make those who haven't received it feel as if they are less Christian. We ask ourselves the question, "What's wrong with us that we are denied this ecstasy?" Is this spiritual envy on our part, Lord?

You know I have even prayed for it! Is there something in me that is blocking the way?

I have always believed that, when my parents brought me to you in Holy Baptism, by your promise and their faith with the water and the

Word, I was the recipient of your Holy Spirit—that was your gift. And then, as I was nurtured in the faith through my childhood years, my awareness of your presence grew, until in confirmation I affirmed for myself the faith my parents had expressed when I was a babe. You have always been with me!

There have been valleys and mountains and monotonous plains, but even in those times when I've ignored you, you've always been there. And the joy of your presence is truly my strength; you keep expanding my horizon and nudging me to become more sensitive to the world's needs. The peace that comes from knowing that, whether I live or die, I am yours makes me face the oncoming years unafraid.

Am I still missing something, Lord? What lesson would you have me be learning?

I remember my parents' faith. Your love in them was so real it reached out to the lonely, the destitute, and the needy. It wasn't spectacular; it was everyday sufficiency, living in the peace of the forgiveness of sins and the joy of loving.

Now as I think about them and the richness of their lives, what more do I want?

They went home to be with you, praising you! Please, Lord, help me to be satisfied with the gifts you've given me and to use them to glorify you! Help me to seek more and more of the gift which you called "the greatest of these"!

Ruth

29

Dear God,

You know I have 19 grandchildren, each as un-alike as can be, and each well loved by you and me and their parents. I'm concerned about them, Lord! It's a messy situation my generation has handed down to them! We're constantly hearing about economic disaster and, more awfully and realistically, the threat of nuclear annihilation. Some of them are very discouraged. What can I say to them? How can I be helpful?

First of all, you've told me words aren't effective unless they are backed by living deeds. I hear you say to me, "Why call me Lord, Lord, and do not the things I say!" Please forgive the many inconsistencies of my life! Give me grace to admit them to you and to them! Give me the courage to be honest about my mistakes and generous about theirs. The lines of communication so quickly get clogged by what people call "the generation gap," whatever that is! Shucks! Is there any gap that love can't bridge over?

They can so easily be overwhelmed by temptations, Lord. Drugs, alcohol, abuse of sex, indolence, self-centeredness, indifference to your love, the desire to be "in," and downright rebellion—all of these are the temptations they face. Up to a point, we faced them, too, but not through television, radio, and movies! They are being battered at from all sides.

First of all, you tell me to surround them with prayer, that even as I lift each one to you, I can know you are answering with your wisdom and love—in your timetable! I can know you are putting forces to work for their eternal welfare and for lives here on this earth that will bless others.

What do I want for my grandchildren, Lord? My human pride says good marks in school, good jobs, happy marriages, or, if they're single, fulfilled lives. Are these what life is all about? Oh, not that these are bad things to hope for—but, if anything, they should be by-products rather than the mainstream. And what is that?

You've made it very clear, and it's the same for young and old! It's to put you first in their lives! Then life abundant will open up as they seek to serve the people of the world. Give me courage to tell them it may be tough going; your way led you to a cross—but what a victory! I want to warn them that they may be ridiculed even by some of their so-called friends! But help them to know your grace is sufficient, that you'll be with them all the way.

O Lord, I want so much for them to know the joy and power of prayer. I want them to find Christian fellowship that will strengthen and encourage them. I want them to know that this grandma will always welcome them no matter what and will do everything in her power to help them.

Here they are, Lord, all 19 of them, each with their own needs. Thank you that I may bring them to you!

Ruth

30

Dear God,

You must get awfully weary of my repetitions and complaints. But again I thank you so much for your patience and for even encouraging me to unburden my heart.

It's the South African-Namibian situation that lays so heavily on my conscience! It came to me afresh in a Christmas letter from one of our missionaries in Tanzania. He deplored the witness to the young emerging African nations, of our country refusing to do anything to help carry out the United Nations agreement of Namibia's independence, as long as Russia and Cuba had people in Angola. What a sardonic hoax such a policy is! A little enslaved nation becomes the pawn of two supreme powers. Lord, I know that kind of thinking is so unlike you that it can't be your will.

From our Namibian Christian friends at the seminary we hear of the persecution and violent destruction they are subjected to. This one friend told us how, while he was preparing a sermon, the South African mercenaries burst into his home and demanded that he come outside. They lined him up along with several of the church leaders and made them stand in the hot sun for three hours, jeering at them and deriding them. Then, before they would release them, they made them jump up and down and say, "I love South Africa!" After he told this he turned to us and said, "What would you do? Had I resisted, I would have been killed. What good would I be to my people then? We carry the glimmer of hope that the countries of the world will see and hear and come to our rescue!" Now that his seminary studies have been completed, he will go back—to what? I hear the refrain: "Is it nothing to you, all you that pass by?"

I'm thankful to you, God, for giving writers inspiration to portray situations and to stir us. Alan Paton's new book *Oh, But Your Land Is Beautiful* is one that deeply moved me. It seemed to me he was really speaking for you when he told of a conversation between a white man and a black man in South Africa. Each of them was putting his life on the line for racial justice and unity. Then the white man turned to his black friend and said, "You know things may be very rough for you. It won't be easy. What is your thinking about that?" And the black man's response was, "Well, I look at it this way. When I get up there, the great Judge will say, 'Where are your scars?' And if I say I haven't any, he will ask, 'Were there no causes worthy of getting scars?' "

Is it, Lord, that we're afraid to take a stand, that we want to protect our own interests over and above our concern for justice?

We so glibly talk about following you. We so heartily sing, "Where you lead us, we will follow!" Where are we when these, your people, suffer such ignominy and servitude? Where are we as your church? Do we protest to our leaders?

You went to the cross—for us—for all humanity! What kind of Milquetoast followers are we?

Lord, inform us, stir us, and give us the faith and love to put our profession into living! God, help Namibia. Use us!

Ruth

31

Dear God,

I can't believe it! Whatever is happening to our responsibility to commitment? I have just been told of another marriage breakup, another parsonage couple getting divorced! The frequency of this kind of news is astounding. What is the trouble, Lord?

And what kind of advice do you give to a mother who is really trying to live your presence in her home but whose husband ridicules her? Their two little boys, caught in the variance of values between their parents, are showing emotional instability and fantasizing. Is it that woman's duty to stick it out or, on behalf of those children, should she break with that union and provide a less contentious atmosphere? When the father is away on trips the boys are relaxed and do better in school. I remember how you put a little child in the midst of the people gathered about you and said to them, "If anyone should cause one of these little ones to lose his faith in me, it would be better for that person to have a large millstone tied around his neck and be drowned in the deep sea" (Matt. 18:6 TEV). We have prayed that the father would come to his senses. Making money seems to be his chief goal. But the boys' disturbances seem to grow worse. Please, God, guide that mother. She loves you and wants your love to dominate her home. And she is so sensitive to the needs of others and so generous and ready to be helpful wherever she can be.

There is another situation that some folks face. What if your partner is unfaithful to you? A woman for the last two years has spent her weekends with another man, one for whom she works, who also is married. Again, there are children. What is the best for them? Lord, invade that home and give direction.

We need you to remind us that even if a mistake has been made, with you there can be a new beginning. We all need that knowledge. Which one of us hasn't erred? We need to be reminded that your presence can work miracles.

Help us to teach our young people that they must work at making a marriage, that husband and wife shouldn't compete, but each should *complete* the other. There is such a good word in your book: "In humility count others better than yourselves" (Phil. 2:3). And we should remember that there is but one head of a household, and that is you!

So many people make their chief goal the outward fixings: a beautiful house, fashionable furnishings, and all the trappings of our civilization. Are these really what make a home?

The director of the World Refugee Service told us the story of a little girl in a refugee camp in Berlin. She was pulling a rag doll in a shoe carton when she was stopped by a tourist who said, "You poor little thing! Isn't it too bad you don't have a home?" The child's quick response was, "Oh, but we do! We have a beautiful home! We just don't have a house to put it in!" What are our values?

There is a place in Germany with an interesting story. Folks don't seem to know if it's fact or fiction. But it has an important point. On the top of a high hill overlooking the city of Weinsberg there is a huge old fortress. At night spotlights shine from it, and it presents quite a spectacle. Townspeople will tell you the story of how, in the days of the feudal lords, a large contingent of an enemy army surrounded the fortress. They sent up word that they would permit the women and children to come out before they sacked it. Further, they stipulated that the women could take out their most valuable possession. Imagine their consternation and surprise when the women marched out with their husbands on their backs!

Lord, those women were ingenious! Help us to ask ourselves, "How precious are our partners?"

Ruth

32

Dear God,

How the time has flown! Your book describes it as "swifter than a weaver's shuttle." I think I mentioned that to you in one of my first letters on this trip. Now I'm going home to the United States, to my family scattered there, to my home church, to my friends, and to my apartment. Yes, and to a heavy schedule of commitments!

As I pack my belongings, I think back to what these two months have held. How you have blessed

us, Lord! We've known your journeying mercies in our trip to Rome, to the Taizè Conference, in our trip along the Danube to Sigmaringen, and then in that fantastic long weekend in Berlin. And everywhere we've experienced the wonder of Christian fellowship—your family in all these different places —across language barriers and national affiliations. You heard us when we were singing your praises in Latin as we crossed the Austrian Alps. You knew what we were singing as our voices (yes, including me with my wheezy alto, blended with the fresh, young voices of the grandchildren) poured out our praise in "Magnificat," "Gloria in Excelsis Deo," "Jubilatè Deo," and the other lovely canons we had learned. Singing together is ageless!

And I felt and saw your presence in the perspective of the vistas of that Danube trip—you the creator of such a beautiful world. And thank you for being so real as we worshiped in the *Marienkirche* in East Berlin. I'll never forget all the young people who were there. Many of them, as you know, have to give up any ambitions about a higher education because they choose to follow you. And thank you for the gracious people who provided such warm hospitality and whom you have used so effectively in the causes of reconciliation, justice, and peace. The symbol of that divided city haunts me, Lord. Help me not to build walls to separate myself from those with whom I disagree but rather to build bridges! Yes, it's been an amazing two months. Thank you! Thank you!

Going home! I can't help but wonder, Lord, when you will be tapping me on the shoulder and bidding me to that final trip home—the one you've prepared! You have shown the way and provided the ticket and you've promised to be with me all the way. I thank you, then, that even that trip, with all of its unknowns, I can anticipate with joy and confidence because of your everlasting love. Yes, even though health may fail (I can feel this body is wearing out), your grace will be sufficient for each day. So I am unafraid!

But, Lord, I pray you will keep me alive to know how I can serve you to the very end of this earthly life. Keep me from coddling my aches and pains; make me aware of how I can be helpful to other people.

And, dear God, give me a grateful heart! The other day I heard such a good story. It was about one of your real friends coming to the pearly gates but being refused entrance by the angel on guard. The heavenly computer hadn't gotten the word through as to his eligibility. So the angel said, "Your name isn't here; you'll have to go to the other place!"

The man, being the kind he was, thought that's really what he deserved when he found himself in hell. Even in the unbearable heat of that environment he kept thanking you for all his blessings. The more he thanked the lower the flames became. His gratitude worked like a fan and cooled off his surroundings. The devil came to him, so the story goes, and said in a very agitated manner, "Get out of here. You're changing the climate!"

You are the great climate changer, Lord. Live in me! And keep me forever grateful!

Ruth

—————— 33 ——————

Dear God,

How can I put into adequate words the power of your presence at that service last night! Lord, you were so obviously there in the opening hymn when we sang of the cross and the costly price you paid for our redemption. You were there in that Old Testament passage from Jeremiah where you talk about the new covenant in which your law would be written in our hearts and where you promise to be our God. You promise we won't have to teach others because all will know you from the least to the greatest—and you will forgive our sins! Thank you for that great word!

And then there was the Epistle Lesson from Hebrews: a reiteration of the Old Testament promise with the additional gift of freedom to enter the Holy Place because of your Son becoming our high priest and opening up this new and living way—the promise of your coming again. The passage was read with such clarity and meaning.

Next there was that young woman who began very timorously but picked up courage as she shared the Gospel Lesson: the story of the Passover observance that established what we call the Lord's Supper. Your presence in an amazing way, carried us back in time and to the place of that memorable event.

So the ground was laid for what followed.

After the offering had been taken, during which there was a simple witness in song, the pastor turned to the people and said: "I want *you* to give the message tonight. While the organ plays softly in the background, think what witness you would like to give of the Lord's presence in your life." Then followed that beautiful time of quiet reflection. How you spoke to me, Lord, about that ugly feeling I tried to put down into a corner of my heart, that feeling toward someone I thought was trying to take advantage of us. And I was ashamed of my smallness of spirit. You know I talked to you about that.

Then it was time for the pastor to call for those who would want to witness. Your spirit was moving among those people. I loved the courage of that first woman who stood up and poured out her gratitude to you for helping her through many difficulties. You remember she thanked you, too, for the family of God that had been such a source of strength. I learned afterwards from the pastor something of her story. Her husband is an alcoholic. You know how difficult he has been. This caused her diabetes to flare up and she had to go to the hospital. While there, her son had an accident that demolished their car, and when she returned home she learned her husband had been to the racetrack and gambled away $900. This is the woman who was pouring out her thanksgiving! Not only that, but the pastor told me she was the one who would find people in the hospital who had no one to care for them, no one to visit them. She would come to him with these names, that he might call on them and share your love. Who but your Spirit could produce a lady like that! There were "Amens" as she finished her testimony!

A young adult then rose to her feet. Didn't you like the fervor with which she spoke when she told about how indifferent she had been to the work of your kingdom and how now she had found a new joy in fellowship and in loving work to do. Her growing knowledge of you had changed her life.

Before she sat down, a young teenager arose and with such fresh enthusiasm told of what her Bible class meant to her and the example of her loving teacher. Her conclusion was: "I wish all the kids out there could have the fun I'm having in trying to help others!"

There were tears when the next one spoke. A very young man rose to say thanks to you and the pastor and the church for helping to spare his tiny baby nephew who was brought to the hospital, starving to death. The doctors had wondered if there were any life left at all in that little bewizened body. But you gave them skill and heard the prayer that was offered. And now, it seemed, the little one was being restored to life. And this very young uncle couldn't say enough thanks to you. I had tears of joy!

It seems as if I'm going on forever, but it wasn't that long because each story was so exciting.

There was the woman who had been in the hospital paralyzed from her neck down with some strange disease. Now she was back in the choir, singing her joy. She was responsible for 13 little children and grandchildren whom she supported by working in a factory. But you know how she gladly gives her tenth to you!

And didn't you like the way the choir director stood up and said: "I want to sing my witness!" And did she ever—with an old gospel song!

How very real you were, Lord, as we were given the bread and the wine. It seemed that across the centuries and around the world that table of loving sacrifice was spread.

Thank you for that beautiful preparation for Easter, that celebration of victory over death.

Thank you for all those people willing to stand up and witness to your power in their lives.

Thank you that I could be there to experience it.

And thanks, Lord, that in your great plan this is but a foretaste of what's to come!

Thank you for great expectations!

Love,
Ruth

34

Dear God,

It's happening to me! I can hardly believe it! How many times I've tried to offer a word of courage and strength to folks in a similar situation! But somehow it's different when it really hits you!

Out of necessity the announcement was casual. How else can a doctor break the news, "You have a tumor"? Momentarily my world was shattered! Outwardly there were few signs as I said, "It isn't too great a surprise. I sort of expected it." But inwardly things began to churn. I got myself out of the office and into my car. I had promised to go to a luncheon, but how should I act? As if nothing had happened? I knew there would be questions. I would try to be casual—maybe just tell a couple of intimate friends. You did keep trying to get

through to me, Lord, but my thoughts were play-ing pandemonium so I didn't hear you for quite some time.

The doctor had urged me to go to the hospital immediately. I told him I couldn't! I had plans and commitments. How could I cancel at this late date? Well, the doctor didn't want to wait too long, so we compromised. I would fulfill some major com-mitments and then check into the hospital.

So on Monday we headed for the hospital. The examination by the specialist there confirmed my doctor's suspicion. It was a malignant tumor. And my heart hasn't been doing so well.

Now three days later and after much blood-drawing and enemas and a liquid diet, I'm to be operated on. You have so consistently covered me with the wings of your Spirit! And yet I've had my dips. But always underneath were your ever-lasting arms. You have been so patient with me.

Now I want to witness to what it means to trust you in such a time, with such a problem. I want to tell the world what freedom there is in being able to say: "Whether I live or die, I am the Lord's."

I love life, Lord, and if you should give me more time, I would want to be about your business. I want to challenge my beloved country to put its trust in you — not in nuclear bombs. I want to challenge people everywhere to be stewards of what you've given them — and for those of us who have been given so much to share our skills and resources and love with those who have so little. What a world that would be — the kind you meant it to be!

But God, if this is the time you tap me on the shoulder, what anticipations are mine! Sometimes I try to imagine the beauty and wonder of it. You've told us that it's beyond our human comprehension, and your Son has shown us the way and opened the gates with his death and resurrection. He has said: "Because I live, you also will live" (John 14:19 TEV), and "I am the resurrection and the life.

Whoever believes in me will live, even though he dies" (John 11:25 TEV).

Thank you for your forgiveness! How infinitely patient you have been with me. Thank you for everlasting life — your free gift through Jesus Christ, *my* Lord. I'm ready, Lord, for whatever tomorrow might hold. Precious Lord, take my hand!

Ruth